Retention Of Culture
As Inequity

Retention Of Culture As Inequity

Dr. Josephine Uzoamaka Aguoji

To order additional copies of this book, contact:
Xlibris Corporation
1-888-795-4274
www.Xlibris.com
Orders@Xlibris.com
48470

Contents

Acknowledgement

I would like to thank my children, Engineer Ifeanyichukwu Aguoji, Tochukwu Aguoji,

Uchenna Aguoji, Chinenye Aguoji and Adaora Aguoji, for their patience.

I thank my husband, Honorable Michael Aguoji, for all his support and assistance.

I also, thank Dr. Donna Wright for the inspiration and making this book a reality.

Geographical/Development of Cultural Beliefs and Disability

One of the primary ways that we limit ourselves as human beings is by the limiting assumptions and negative beliefs we hold. Some of these beliefs may have made sense at the time we adopted them, but when we continue to hold onto them long after our environment has changed, they become maladaptive and even toxic. Much of what we call culture is the outcome of how we relate to our physical environment and our sense of responsibility toward the human beings among whom we live and with and the rest of creation around us. Our very physical form is disparaged, and people are simply exploited, ignored, dehumanized for no other reason than that they are disabled.

Primitive ideas that people who look or are different are not quite human still rules the minds of most Nigerians. All human beings are children of God. The injustice built into global economic relations that exploit sectors of the human race by the way they look and their gender disputes the integrity of humanity.

All of us are cultural beings; we all have culture, and our culture shapes how we see the world and make sense of it. Our culture influences our behaviors and interactions. Our culture mediates how we make sense of disability and respond to people with disabilities. Culture is not static; it is constantly challenging and responding to shifting environments and circumstances. Within each culture there are many subcultures, which means that not all beliefs, values, attitudes, and behaviors are shared among all people of one cultural group.

African culture is mostly dominated by able-bodied males, as is the culture of many nations worldwide.

The paternalistic propensity of African culture, especially in Nigeria, the Igbo culture, does not indicate subjugation of people with disability.

Nigeria is located in West Africa situated along the eastern coast of the Gulf of Guinea. More than 250 ethnic tribes live in Nigeria. The three largest and most dominant ethnic groups are Hausa, Yoruba, and the Igbo however, there are other smaller groups, which include the Fulani, Ijaw, Kanuri, Ibibio, Tiv, and the Edos.

There are three main environmental regions, savannah, tropical forest, and coastal wetlands, which greatly affects the cultures of the people who live in Nigeria.

The dry, open grasslands of the savannah make cereal farming and herding a way of life for the Hausas and the Fulani.

The wet tropical forests to the south are good for farming; fruits and vegetables are main income produce for the Yoruba, Igbo, and others residing in this area. The small ethnic groups living along the coast such as Ijaw and the Kalabarai are forced to keep their villages small due to lack of dry land.

The Rivers Niger and Benue joined together in the center of the country, creating a Y that splits Nigeria into three separate parts. The Y marks the boundaries of the three major ethnic groups, with Hausa in the north, the Yoruba in the southwest, and the Igbo in the southeast. English is the official language of Nigeria, used in all and everyday interactions.

When children reach the age of about four or five, they often are expected to start performing a share of the household duties. As the children get older, their responsibilities grow. Young men are expected to help their fathers in the fields or tend the livestock.

Young women help with the cooking, fetch water, or do laundry. These tasks help the children learn how to become productive members of their family and community.

As children, many Nigerians learn that laziness is not acceptable; everyone is expected to contribute.

Nigerian ethnic groups' education of children is a community responsibility.

In the Igbo culture, the training of children is the work of both men and women, within the family and outside the family.

Neighbors usually look after youngsters while parents may be busy with other chores.

It is not unusual to see a man or woman disciplining a child who is not his own. A child becomes a member of the human race through becoming first a member of a family. His/her birth heralds joy and self-fulfillment for both parents because children according to African traditional beliefs are gifts from God. The presence of a disabled child brings grief and sadness to the parents. This is usually an expected reaction for every parent whose wish is to give birth to a normal child. The parents' attitude may negatively change; hence, the love and care that the child needs for development may be lacking. Research has shown that in Igbo culture, before colonization, people afflicted with any form of disability were thought to be cursed by gods. They were viewed as the dregs of the society and of bad omens. In the past and even today, the family of a child with a disabling condition tries to keep the affliction a secret, and as a result such a child will likely be kept away from the public. All Nigerian children are supposed to have access to a local elementary school. Thus, the government aims to provide universal free primary education for both boys and girls. The number of girls in class is usually much lower than the number of boys twenty years ago, though the case is different now. Sending every child in a family to school can often put a lot of strain on a family. The family will lose the child's help around the house during school hours and will have to pay for uniforms and supplies. If parents are forced to send one child to school over another, many Igbo parents will choose to educate a male child before a female child. African, especially Igbo, culture is mostly male-dominated, as is the culture of many native nations worldwide. The paternalistic propensity of African or Igbo culture does not indicate subjugation of women or people with disability.

People are constantly evaluating and making judgments about other people and events. We react to people and situations on the basis of how we evaluate and judge them. History is replete with examples of disabled people worldwide being ridiculed, killed, abandoned to die, or condemned to permanent exclusion in asylums (Pritchard 1963).

Anang (1992) claims that the Greeks abandoned their disabled babies on hillsides to die while early Chinese left their disabled people to drown in rivers. In Europe, Nero Commodus is said to have targeted bow and arrows on physically disabled individuals and the church in discrimination against women and people with disability remained a problem; female genital mutilation remained widely practiced in some parts of the country; and child abuse, child prostitution, and child labor were common. People with disability were not seen as equal to other children. They are widely disregarded as both capable of and needing, love, affection, humor, friendship, cultural, artistic expression, and intellectual stimulation. The people with disability were segregated, marginalized (which serves to express the experience of subordination in the lives of the people with disability), isolated, and can be subjected to physical and sexual violence with relative impunity. Usually they are defined by what they lack rather than what they have. This process not only dehumanizes people with disability but also dehumanizes the society.

A human rights group outlined the atrocities meted out against the Osu in Igbo land. They include (1) poisoning of children by parents, (2) disinheritance, ostracism, organized attack, heaping harvest offering separately in churches, denial of membership in social clubs, violent disruption of marriage ceremonies, deprivation of property, and expulsion of wives.

The Osu caste discrimination is very pronounced in the area of marriage. An Osu cannot marry a freeborn. The belief is that any freeborn that marries an Osu defiles the family.

So freeborn families are always up in arms against any of their members who want to marry an Osu. They go to any length to scuttle the plan. Because of the Osu factor, marriages in Igbo land are preceded by investigations, elders on both sides travel to native villages to find out the social status of the other party.

Having an Osu identity is like leprosy in the minds of my people. The belief in and practice of the Osu caste system continue to wax strong in Igbo land. Recently, I learned of a beautiful young lady whose husband deserted her after having three children. The husband had abandoned her with three children after ten years of marriage because the lady was an Osu. There have been several instances like that where a young man and woman of Igbo origin has suffered heartbreak and emotional traumas as a result of this cultural disease.

And now the question is, why is it that this cultural practice has refused to go away even among educated Igbos?

The reason is not far-fetched.

The practice of Osu caste system is hinged on religion, supernaturalism, and theism. And Igbo's are deeply religious and theistic people. The Osu are regarded as unclean or untouchable because they are alleged to be dedicated to the gods. So it is the dedication to the gods that makes the Osu status a condition of permanent and irreversible disability and stigma.

So this cruel custom will not be eradicated until Igbos begin to realize that gods are imaginary beings, not objective entities. Igbos need to understand that deities and spirits are mental constructs used to control and organize the society at the infancy of the human race.

Some cultural beliefs have been found to be a major factor. All the ethnic groups in Nigeria have one belief or the other against persons with special needs. Some believe that they are reincarnated beings, while others believe they are a result of the sins committed by their parents to the "gods" of the land, so they are treated as outcasts and are denied their fundamental human rights. With civilization, awareness, and advancement, views of the people are changing toward these children, but at a slow rate.

Each culture has its own unique characteristics which usually are best understood by indigenous people. Community attitudes are an expression of a people's culture. A study of some aspects of culture ought to reveal generally held views about disability and disabled people. These aspects may include customs, paintings, drawings, carvings, and the folklore and language used in relation to disability and disabled persons and folklore. Ingastad (1990) provides a hint in this direction when she writes:

In the old days in Europe a disabled family member was considered a shame, a sign of God's punishment and thus someone to be hidden, killed etc. This may have been true to some extent, but if we go to what is probably our best source, folktales and literature, we get a different picture. (p.188)

An examination of attitudes toward the disabled across cultures suggests that societal perceptions and treatment of the disabled are neither homogenous nor static (Roeher, 1961). Greek and Roman perceptions of disability and illness are reflected in the literature. Among the Greeks, the sick were considered inferior (Barker et al., 1980), and in his *Republic*, Plato recommended that the deformed offspring of both the superior and inferior be put away in some "mysterious unknown place" (Goldberg & Lippman, 1998, p. 199).

However, early Christian doctrine introduced the view that disease is not a disgrace nor a punishment by special supernatural agents. These children were well received since they were believed to bring good luck (Wright, 1996). Nnabagwu (1977) observed that among the Ibos of Nigeria, treatment of the disabled varied from pampering to total rejection.

Diversification in perceptions of the disabled exists in Ghana as it does in other places in Africa. Among the Ashanti of Central Ghana, traditional beliefs preclude men with physical defects such as amputations from becoming chiefs, as evident in the destooling of a chief if he acquires epilepsy (Nnabagwu, 1977; Sarpong, 1974). Children with obvious deviations were unacceptable; for example, an infant born with six fingers was killed upon birth (Nnabagwu, 1977). Severely retarded children were abandoned on riverbanks or near the sea so that such "animal-like children" could return to what was believed to be their own kind (Danquah, 1977). In contrast, the Ga, a group from the Accra region of Ghana, treated the so-called feeble-minded with awe. They believed the "retarded" to be the reincarnation of a deity. Hence, the latter were always treated with the greatest kindness, gentleness, and patience (Facia,1994).

The degree to which the disabled are accepted within a society is not directly proportionate to its financial resources. Lippman (1972) observed that in many instances, small European countries such as Denmark and Sweden were accepting of their disabled individuals. He also found that these countries provided more effective rehabilitation services. The prevalent philosophy in Scandinavian countries is acceptance of social responsibility for all members of society without regard for the type or degree of disabling condition.

While throughout the world many changes have occurred in the status and treatment of the disabled, the residue of tradition and past belief influences present-day practices affecting this group (DuBrow, 1965; Wright, 1996). Thomas (1980) sees societal perception and treatment of the disabled within and across cultural boundaries as a kaleidoscope of varying hues, reflecting tolerance, hatred, stigmatization, love, fear, awe, reverence, and revulsion. The most consistent feature in the treatment of the disabled in most societies is that they are categorized. "Deviance, rather than being an innate characteristic of the individual, is an attribute defined by society" (Lippman, 1972, p. 206).

Richardson et al. (1996) examined the effect of rate characteristics on attitude valence relating to disability. Hundreds of ten- and eleven-year-old children with diverse backgrounds were tested for their preference ranking of six stimulus pictures, one of which showed a nondisabled child, each of the five others depicting a child with one type of physical handicap or another. Regardless of race, sex, socioeconomic status, and other similar characteristics, the rater subjects showed a high preference for the normal child, a lesser preference for children with mild disability, and the least preference for those with disabilities whose appearance was less attractive. From this raters' consistency in ranking, the investigators conclude that a cultural uniformity in reactions existed toward persons with physical disability.

Follow-up studies and replications of the 1961 investigation have yielded data that support the initial findings (Richardson, 1983, 1996). One other source of insight into the nature of public attitudes is the attitude research that examined not only a particular group, but also comparable groups or various segments of which a group is composed. Two such research studies cited below contribute some of the clearest findings on public attitudes. To ascertain the attitudes harbored toward deaf individuals by different age groups within the American culture, Horowitz, Rees, and Horowitz (1992) administered attitude questionnaires to five groups composed of twenty subjects each: sixth-grade students, high school students, undergraduate students, graduate students, and members of a parent-teacher association.

The results showed that the five groups formed a continuum of increasing maturity and sophistication in attitudes, given the respondents' views, toward the deaf's personal and achievement characteristics. The groups, however, did not differ in their views on training for the deaf and treatment of the deaf individual. Gottlief and Corman (1998) administered attitude instruments to a population of 430 respondents to measure awareness—through semantic differential and attitudinal rating—and to appraise public acceptance of disabled children. The results showed that on some scale items, the respondents were massively positive in attitudes while on some items they were not; some segments of the population also evidenced more favorability than others on given issues. Whereas 88 percent of the respondents agreed that parents ought to allow their normal children to play with disabled peers, the population was fairly even divided on the three response alternatives—agree, disagree, unsure—regarding whether the disabled child should be educated in a special class. In addition, older respondents, parents of school-age children, and persons who previously had contact with the disabled were more inclined to favor segregation of children with disabilities in the community.

These studies, no doubt, provide valuable insight into the nature of cultural beliefs. But it is unclear why the findings differ so much among many of the cited studies. The results obtained by Golin (1997), Richardson et al. (1996), Horowitz, Rees, and Horowitz (1992), and Gottlieb and Corman (1998), in particular and taken together, indicate that public beliefs toward the disabled are sometimes positive, sometimes negative, and sometimes neutral or mixed. However, one cannot as yet confidently pinpoint what factor leads to which belief propensity—the particular conditions experimentally created by the investigator, the type of attitude instrument used in a study, the nature of social intercourse with the disabled, which attitude subjects perceived was implicated in the study exercise, and so forth. Even more difficult to evaluate are any effects the instruments employed had on the study outcome because most of these studies used (sometimes understandably) nonstandardized scales whose psychometric properties were usually not reported. Based on the assumption that people with disabilities could not care for themselves, many were institutionalized or placed in nursing homes, while others were excluded by inaccessible buildings or by people without disabilities who regarded them as subhuman (Robert, 1994; Rodde, 1999). Legal reforms have included the Americans with Disabilities Act of 1990, which acknowledges "historically" that society has tended to isolate and segregate individuals with disabilities. Despite some improvements, such forms of discrimination against individuals who have experienced prejudice on the basis of race, color, sex, national origin, age, or disability have often had no legal recourse to redress such discrimination (U.S. Congress, 1990).

One variable consists of the values and beliefs of different ethnic and cultural groups, as suggested in *Attitudes towards Disabilities in a Multicultural Society*. Different ethnic and cultural groups have different taboos, which can be reflected in their attitudes toward a certain type of disability. What is unacceptable in one group, such as physical disabilities or AIDS, might be acceptable in a different cultural group or moderately tolerated in another. Yet it is not as simple as one group being less willing to feel pity for a person with a disability than another group. One might generalize that people with hidden disabilities, such as diabetes or chronic fatigue syndrome, are accepted more readily by society than people with visible disabilities such as cerebral palsy. However, while mental illness and AIDS can also be considered hidden disabilities, attitudes toward these types of disability can be more negative than attitudes toward someone with polio or muscular dystrophy (Legge, & Pennay,

1998). The purpose of *Attitudes towards Disabilities in a Multicultural Society* was to determine cultural attitudes that affect medical service to patients in Australia. Different ethnic groups had different beliefs and attitudes toward disabilities that could affect their rights and willingness to seek treatment or rehabilitation services.

Weller, Costeff, Cohen, and Ratiman (1974) investigated the effects of cultural background and socioeconomic status of parents and the severity of the child's handicap on parents' perceptions of disability, their guilt feelings, and acceptance of the child with disability. Interviewed in this study were seventy-six Israeli mothers of children with mental retardation whose ethnic background was Middle Eastern or European. The results showed that parents of children with disabilities, in contrast to those whose children were retarded, evidenced more realistic perceptions of their children's capabilities. Whereas the degree of retardation and the parents' social class—not their cultural background—affected perceptions of retardation, they affected neither parental guilt feelings nor acceptance/rejection of the child with disability.

The data above lend support to Wolfensberger and Kurtz's (1971) finding that parents from a higher social class were more realistic than those from a lower class in appraising the ability of a child with disability. The data also support the finding that attitude-behavior tends to pattern in the same ordered way across nations and cultures (Vurgelja-Maglajlic & Jordan, 1974). Jordan and Friesen's (1968) cross-cultural study of the attitudes of professionals, however, suggests some sense in which attitudes toward the disabled are affected by differences in culture. To this extent, much more data than are available now will be needed to determine where similarities and differences lie in the disability attitudes of parents—versus nonparents—within the same culture as well as across cultures.

If parents with higher socioeconomics status are more realistic in their beliefs and attitudes, they may not be more accepting of a disabled child than their lower-SES counterparts. According to Nieves-Torres (1983), who studied parents in Puerto Rico, parents in the higher-SES group, compared to lower-SES parents, tended more to reject and overprotect their disabled children. Such overprotectiveness and rejection appeared to negatively affect the social competence of disabled children, especially when the child possessed an IQ in the low twenty to thirty-five range. Data reported by Evans (1996), Gottlieb and Corman (1975), Nieves-Torres (1983), and Vurdelja-Maglajlic and Jordan (1974) suggest that parents are more positive than the general public in their beliefs and attitudes toward disabled children. In particular, parents with disabled siblings, compared to other parents, evidence greater favorability in evaluative attitudes and community acceptance of disabled children.

Another distinct feature of the disability movement is the cultural versus medical model viewpoint. As Shapiro (1994) notes, those members of the disability movement wanted to be accepted as they were, not to be subjected to "fixing" or correcting a condition that was not part of the mainstream population. The disability movement states that one be fully accepted, with diversity being a positive attribute (Heumann, 1994). Recent activities such as the increase in sports involvement, technological advances, and media promotion have placed disability groups in the mainstream of society, emphasizing the many accomplishments they have achieved.

Shapiro (1994) discusses how the current movement toward self-determination has been the outgrowth of advocacy groups that formed at the end of the nineteenth century, especially those for deaf and blind individuals. Later, the Civil Rights Act of 1968 would fight discrimination of gender, race, or religion; the civil rights movement would become a model for many disability groups who currently identify with aspects of that movement.

During the same year, the Architectural Barriers Act of 1968 ensured physical access to federal buildings. Ward (1996) cites the disability rights movement as having grown out of the 1960s independent living movement that aligned, as noted above, with the civil rights movement. People with disabilities at that time were socially and politically motivated to foster change in their lives. Then, the need to change the public image of the "handicapped" was conceived. People with disabilities mobilized, using basic precepts that minority groups used in their quest for equal opportunity. The Vocational Rehabilitation Act of 1973 was passed to prohibit discrimination against persons with disabilities in the federal government. Section 504 of the act would be the basis for the Americans with Disabilities Act of 1990.

The growth of the disability rights movement culminated in the Americans with Disabilities Act of 1990. This act, known as ADA, expanded on the Vocational Rehabilitation Act of 1975. It was one of the most significant legislative acts in its implications for self-determination of individuals with disabilities. According to the Americans with Disabilities Act of 1990, PL 101-336 (July 26, 1990), Title 42, U.S.C. 12101 et seq.: U.S. Statutes at Large, 104, 327-328, the term "disability" is defined as a mental or physical impairment that substantially limits one or more major life activities; a record of such an impairment; being regarded as having an impairment. The ADA prohibits discrimination on the basis of disability in the following areas:

Title I: Employment—prohibits discrimination against a qualified individual with a disability in hiring, discharging, promotion, compensation, and job training.

Title II: Public Services—state and local government departments
and agencies were prohibited from discrimination against
qualified individuals with disabilities in excluding them
from participating in services programs or activities.

Title III: Public Accommodation—an individual with a disability is
protected from discrimination in public accommodations.

Title IV: Telecommunications—a 24-hour TDD voice relay system
and closed captioning of federally funded programs were
established.

As Shapiro (1994) states that these laws were necessary because society
failed to provide for the needs of the disabled and enable them to live to their
optimum capacity. Heumann (1994) cites the progress that has occurred for the
disabled in the twentieth century. Ward (1996) states that if the disabled are
to be independent and self-determined, they must learn from other minority
groups by taking pride in their culture and history. The expansion of the
number of persons with disabilities involved in the disability rights movement
has empowered them and acknowledged them through public awareness. Most
important was the change in disabilities groups.

Now that the disabled have increased their self-determination skills, they
are informing society that persons with disabilities do not want patronizing,
pity or admiration. They want basic respect and increased opportunities
to connect with their community in order to participate fully in daily life.
Through empowerment, they are sensitizing society to the rights of the disabled
(Shapiro, 1994).

On the other hand, the civil rights movement had a significant influence on
the disability rights movement and on the education of students with disabilities.
Deaf and blind persons were the first to form national advocacy organizations.
The deaf culture movement often alludes to the empowerment that was gained
by the movement, and uses it as a model for their own community. Similarly,
organizations for the blind have used both political and legislative means to
gain full access. According to Shapiro (1994), civil rights legislation for the
disabled grew out of the history of oppression of minority groups, which resulted
in those groups demanding their rights through political means. The following
brief summary cites the key accomplishments of the civil rights movement in
an effort to see the commonalities between the movements.

The civil rights movement was the outgrowth of years of racial inequality,
segregation, and discrimination in the United States. Historically, color and
disability were predictors of poverty, particularly under the Jim Crow laws
(Mithaug, 1996). One of the major goals of the civil rights movement was to
end racial segregation and to ensure equal opportunity for all. With the passing
of the Civil Rights Acts, various rights were won. In 1866, the act gave former

slaves the right to hold property; in 1870, the act forbids restrictions on the access of former slaves to public places.

Constitutional amendments further addressed the issues of segregation and discrimination. The Thirteenth Amendment abolished slavery; the Fourteenth Amendment provided for equal protection under the law; the Fifteenth Amendment gave the right to vote to all people. Under these laws, the disenfranchised hoped to achieve social, political, and economic rights for all people. However, despite these amendments and acts, discrimination continued to flourish as a result of Supreme Court decisions that interpreted these constitutional acts in their narrowest meanings while also not defending black rights.

The landmark case of *Plessy v. Ferguson* (1896), in which the Supreme Court would not overturn a Southern policy that prohibited African Americans from riding in segregated railroad cars, found that legal decisions based on race were not in violation of constitutional laws. As a result of these inadequacies, in the early part of the twentieth century, prominent African Americans organized the National Association for the Advancement of Colored People (NAACP), which sought to challenge through the courts major violations of their civil rights (Mithaug, 1996).

In 1954, the Supreme Court ruled in *Brown v. Board of Education* that separate education is not equal education, and steps toward desegregation of schools would follow as a result of this ruling. According to Mithaug (1996), this case resulted in a social upheaval, changing the legal status of African Americans from that of begging to becoming a part of society with equal treatment under the law. Also in 1954, *Plessy v. Ferguson* was overturned with a statement that segregation was inherently unfair to black children.

In 1955, the Jim Crow laws of segregated busing resulted in the Montgomery boycott and the establishment of the Civil Rights Commission. The 1965 Voting Rights Act authorized federal judges to protect African Americans who were prevented from registering to vote. This act empowered African Americans who won social justice by fighting on their own (Mithaug, 1996).

Thus, the Civil Rights Act of 1964 was the result of the civil rights movement of the 1950s and tremendously influenced the current disability rights movement. Many members of the disability rights movement view themselves as having similar issues that minority groups had in their fight for equal opportunity in all aspects of their lives (Shapiro, 1994). The Civil Rights Act of 1964 has eleven titles that prohibit discrimination on the basis of race or color or national origin. Some of the specific titles refer to voting rights (Title I), public accommodation (Title II), public education (Title IV), and fair employment opportunities (Title VII). The 1965 Voting Rights Act banned all forms of racial discrimination in voting. In 1968, the Fair Housing Act made it illegal for property owners and agents to discriminate on the basis of race or color.

While the Civil Rights Act provided for more opportunities for minority groups than ever before, a disregard for specific titles of the act resulted in litigation when personal civil rights were violated. These lawsuits would involve discrimination in housing, education, or employment, and would culminate in further precedent-setting decisions that attempted to ensure compliance with the federal law.

Stereotypic Beliefs about People with Disability

Stereotypes are often the principal identifying characteristic for a person from a particular culture and distort further understanding of that culture. Yet we all make sense of the world and our place in the world through identifying with parts of the community.

In Nigeria, the literature on stereotypical beliefs and rights beliefs has focused on the public attitude toward the disabled. However, very little has been said about people with disability or the relationship between stereotypical beliefs and rights beliefs. Thus, this area of special education represents a neglected domain of research.

A child in Nigeria becomes a member of the human race simply by first becoming a member of a family. His or her birth heralds joy and self-fulfillment for both parents because children, according to traditional African beliefs, are gifts from God. By contrast, the presence of a disabled child brings grief and sadness to the parents. This is usually an expected reaction for every parent whose wish is to have a normal child. The parents' attitude may change for the negative and, thus, the love and care that the child needs for development may be lacking. Research has shown that in Ibo culture, before colonization, people afflicted with any form of disability were thought to be cursed by the gods. They were viewed as the dregs of society and as bad omens. In the past, but even today, the family of a child with a disabling condition tries to keep the affliction a secret, and consequently, such a child will likely be kept away from the public.

The society's perceptions of impairment and disability are colored by a deep-rooted psychological fear of the unknown, the anomalous, and the abnormal (Douglas, 1966). It is widely acknowledged, however, that perceptions of normality are partly, if not wholly, determined by others through learning and the natural transmission of ideology and culture. Here, ideology and culture refer to a communally accepted set of values and beliefs which influences individual perceptions (Douglas, 1966). Throughout history, illness has often been regarded as a form of punishment imposed for wrongdoing (Murdock, 1980). Plagues, paralysis, and blindness are just some of the retributions imposed by divine powers on sinning people as illustrated in the Oedipal myth. In cultural precursors to our own society, however, there is evidence of a consistent bias against disability and disabled people's rights, an issue which has only recently been seriously challenged. Examples can be found in religion, Greek philosophy, and European drama and art since well before the Renaissance. Throughout the Middle Ages, disabled people have been the subject of superstitious beliefs, persecution, and rejection. Haffter (1968) has pointed out that in medieval Europe, disability was associated with evil beliefs and witchcraft. Deformed and disabled children were seen as "changelings" or the devil's substitutes for human children, the outcome of their parents' involvement with the black arts or sorcery.

Shakespeare's *Richard III* illustrates clearly the attitudes that would be experienced by someone born into a world which placed a high premium upon physical normality. Shakespeare portrays Richard as twisted in both body and mind.

> Cheated of feature by dissembling nature,
> Deformed, unfinished, sent before my time
> Into this breathing world, scarce half made up,
> And that so lamely and unfashionable
> The dogs bark at me as I halt by them.

In Ibo land of Nigeria, beliefs of society toward disabled persons in general have been slow to change. The disabled were thought to be the "root of social evils" and a burden to civilization (Swanson & Willis, 1979). However, in the modern democracy, freedom and inclusion are ideals that are the core of the value system.

While modern democracy claims to treat all persons equally, the poor, the disabled, and minority groups have historically been neglected, mistreated, and socially isolated. All of these groups yearned for their rights. They wanted to have the same opportunities for living optimally that more advantaged members of society have experienced. The freedom ideal, which states that every person has the right to determine his or her direction in life, and the inclusion ideal, which states that every person has a right to be included in society, has attempted to allow the disenfranchised the attainment of these benefits.

By following the precepts of these ideals, individuals will become more self-determined, gaining the right of individuals to set goals and to determine the steps necessary to achieve these goals. These ideals will allow individuals to determine their place in the community of their choice.

Stereotypical Beliefs about Disability

Among many of the social experiments attempted in education, one of the most challenging and perplexing has been the commitment to the education of all educable disabled children and adults. The reason underlying this is that the notions regarding physical disabilities and health impairments were closely linked to stereotypical beliefs such as mysticism, occultism, and spiritism.

These traditional misconceptions, beliefs, and prejudices are similar in terms of attitudes toward disabled children among the various ethnic groups in Nigeria. The same applies to a child born deaf or blind. When all efforts at explanation fail, Nigerians are left with no choice but to attribute the cause to stereotypical beliefs and supernatural powers, and to view the child as an agent of the devil and the angry gods.

People with disabilities have experienced, and continue to experience, difficult and degrading existences because of social isolation, underemployment, unemployment, pity, and dependence. Throughout most of the history of the United States, enough evidence can be found of inhospitable treatment of people with disabilities (Shapiro, 1993; Ward, 1996). Citizens who experience cognitive, mental, or physical disabilities have traditionally represented the hidden minority (Percy, 1989; Ward, 1996). Literally through institutionalization and subtly through negative attitudes and behaviors, individuals with disabilities have been isolated from mainstream society and denied the benefits and opportunities available to people without disabilities (Ward, 1996). According to Funk (1987), "Throughout time, the inferior economic and social status of people with disabilities has been viewed as the inevitable consequence of the physical and mental differences imposed by disability" (p. 7). The difficult experiences of people with disabilities are, as Mithaug (1996) states, "a consequence of inequality which leads to unequal prospects for engaging and succeeding in life pursuits" (p. 1).

In the so-called third world countries, the conditions of people with disabilities appear to be worse than those of their counterparts in industrialized nations in terms of health, education, employment, and opportunities to participate fully in their respective societies and to become independent individuals. Negative attitudes, including stereotyping, misconceptions, ignorance, taboos, to name a few, have been frequently cited as the common sociocultural traits responsible for the predicament of people with disabilities. For example, tribal and religious beliefs continue to influence people's thoughts and actions in such a way that those with disabilities are viewed as useless, as being afflicted by sins committed by their ancestors, as bad omens. They consequently are rejected and abandoned. Khalfan (1994), referring to the circumstances of people with disabilities in the third world, explained:

> People with disabilities are caught up in a vicious cycle with regard
> to education and literacy. Many people, including those who are
> disabled, think of disability as being an individual misfortune or as
> a punishment for past sins or as a curse. Society as a whole regards
> disabled people as "useless." (p. 4)

Facia (1994), a social worker from Benin Republic in West Africa, also described the circumstances of people with disabilities in that part of the world:

> Handicapped children have long been considered bearers of a
> curse or recipients of divine wrath at the misdeeds of their parents.
> In some regions, they are killed at birth, or kept well hidden at
> home. But others are treated as gods by their families, unknown to
> outsiders. (p. 8)

In Nigeria, disabled individuals depend on their families, charity, and organized philanthropy. They attend segregated schools which have very limited capacities to enroll all those who are eligible to attend schools. Their lives are virtually controlled by these agencies, as has been true in the United States as well. According to Wehmeyer (1996):

> From cradle to grave, people with disabilities are reliant upon
> dependency-creating systems—educational systems, rehabilitation
> systems, family systems—to meet their needs. As a result, many
> people with disabilities fail to reach maximum levels of independence,
> productivity, inclusion and self-sufficiency outcomes that ironically
> are the main objectives of most of such systems. (p. 18)

These dependency systems generate and promote "learned helplessness," which appears to be the universal experience of people with disabilities and is more acute in developing countries. Feeling a lack of control over one's life and believing that nothing one does makes a difference can lead to what is referred to as "learned helplessness" (Brown, Belz, Corsi, & Wenig, 1993).

Theories of Attitude Formation

Many theories have focused on identifying techniques that produce attitudinal change toward people with disabilities. The results of these theories vary (Donaldson, 1994). For instance, in most studies, structured direct contact with people with disabilities led to a consistent positive attitude change (McHale & Simeonsson, 1980; Voeltz, 1982). Information about disabilities can change attitudes toward people with disabilities, but information alone is not enough (Yuker, 1994). According to Murray-Siller (1984), "to be effective, efforts to change attitudes must incorporate a behavior change component, non-disabled students should not only discuss disability, but also should be involved in regularly repeated interaction with disabled peers" (p. 46).

Attitudes toward people with disabilities are difficult to change, and recent available data do not indicate which procedures are most effective in changing attitudes (Shaver, & Strong, 1989). As noted in a study by Favazza and Odom (1997), behavioral observations need to be included in studies of children's attitudes toward their peers with disabilities, because without these behavioral observations, one cannot determine if changes in children's attitudes are reflected in their behaviors toward their peers with disabilities. It is necessary to learn how and if attitudinal changes toward people with disabilities occur for a particular group of people in a particular environment.

An attitude is made up of cognition, affect, and behavior. The cognitive component of an attitude is an individual's beliefs. The affective component of an attitude is an individual's feelings. The behavioral component is comprised of an individual's behavioral intentions and overt behaviors (Siperstein, 1996). While a great deal of research has assessed the attitudes of nondisabled persons toward those with disabilities, a more limited amount of work has contested theoretical assumptions to further understand the processes that lead to attitudinal change (Donaldson, 1994).

According to the Lewinian theory of attitude change (Lewin, 1995), attitude modification takes place when one's present attitude is unbalanced. This unbalancing occurs when either the restraining forces or the driving forces that hold together an opinion are either increased or decreased. When this equilibrium results, a person's attitude can be altered (Donaldson, 1994). In 1996, Evans' study, based on the Lewinian theory on attitudinal change, found that people without disabilities were uneasy when interacting with people who had disabilities, and this uneasiness created and maintained their negative attitudes. Evans believed that this discomfort during an interaction was the "restraining force" that would not permit a positive attitudinal change. He hypothesized that if people without disabilities could articulate their feelings about disabilities, and if they were provided with models on how to interact with a disabled person, then the "restraining force" would be lifted and attitudinal change could occur (Donaldson, 1994).

This hypothesis was tested in a study using three groups of college students, who were first surveyed to learn their attitudes toward people with disabilities. The students in the experimental group participated in an experimental manipulation administered during contact with a confederate who had a disability; one control group interacted with the same confederate, but with no manipulation; and the other control group interacted with a confederate without a disability. The experimental group interacted individually with a woman who was blind; during this interaction, the blind woman spoke of her feelings about blindness and of other people's curiosity about her blindness. In each interaction, she included three statements: one invited questions about being blind since she did not mind answering questions on this topic; the second stated that she felt being blind had certain social advantages; and the third dealt with her acceptance of the usage of everyday words such as "look," "watch," and "see." One control group interacted with the same blind woman, while the third group interacted with a woman without a disability; however, both sessions remained factual and did not discuss disabilities.

Results indicated that the experimental group's attitudes toward people with disabilities were significantly more positive than the other two groups'. This important finding can be used in very practical ways. People with disabilities can reduce strain and discomfort for people without disabilities during interactions that can ultimately lead to positive changes in the latter group (Evans, 1996). A theoretical model to help understand attitudes toward persons with disabilities was suggested in Asch's (1996) research. In his theory of interpersonal perception, he demonstrated that some personal traits within a pattern of traits were "central" while others were "peripheral." Central traits produced fundamental changes in the entire impression of the person and largely determined others' evaluations of him or her.

Another study that supports this Lewinian theory of attitudinal change toward people with disabilities was done by Langer et al. (1976). These researchers hypothesized that people avoided interaction with individuals with disabilities because they were inclined to stare at them as novel stimuli, but they acknowledge that staring at another person is not socially acceptable. However, when subjects were "allowed" to stare at someone with a disability, they were more likely to interact with that person during any contact (Donaldson, 1994). These findings of all these studies support the idea that if the restraining force toward attitude change is reduced, positive attitudinal change is more likely.

Another theory on why attitudes toward people with disabilities may change is based on empathy. To test this theory, Clore (1992) conducted a simulation study in which experimental subjects without disabilities either acted as role players with disabilities or observers of these role players. The role players followed a specific route in a wheelchair, and the observers followed a role player at a distance of twenty feet. The role players and observers had significantly more positive attitudes toward people with disabilities that were maintained for four months following the study. Clore believed that when the role players and observers noted the reactions of strangers without disabilities to the role players, their empathetic understanding of what it was like to have a disability was enhanced. If a person's attitude toward people with disabilities is to change, the experience needs to be "stranger" than any "restraining force" may be. Also, if people are to perceive clearly how they should react to people with disabilities, they may become more empathetic and change their negative attitudes.

Crandell (cited in Newman & Simpson, 1983) also presented a theory of attitudinal change relating to people with disabilities. He theorized that the cognitive knowledge provided about people with disabilities is more appealing than the actual experience with people with disabilities. This suggests that people who only receive information about individuals with disabilities would have more positive attitudes toward them than people who had actual contact with individuals with disabilities.

According to Siperstein (1996), attitude change results when the three components (cognitive, affective, and behavioral) of an attitude enter into a state of incongruity. When a person's beliefs, feelings, and behavioral intentions are imbalanced, then attitude change will result. When one component of an attitude changes, it affects the other two components. This theory is based on the early work of Heider (1946). As stated in Siperstein (1996), Heider's theory on attitudinal change suggests a relationship between three elements—the person, the other person, and the object—all from the point of view of the first person. The person perceives his/her relationship with the other person and object as either balanced or imbalanced. When someone's attitude is changed, either a balance or an imbalance is created in the system. Efforts to understand attitudes toward disabled persons are reflected in the various theories about able-bodied persons with whom individuals with disabilities interact: namely, the general public, parents, and peers. A cross-section of these studies is presented below.

Society has its own expectations about individuals, which are based on beliefs. To some extent, society shapes what a person may become, depending on the extent to which the society may have provided experience. In Nigeria, disability is often not considered objectively in a social value judgment. Some "handicaps" are socially imposed limitations placed on persons who may be sufficiently different from others, and society itself is part of the problems that disabled people face. For instance, in the construction of public and private buildings, no consideration is given to the accommodation of the disabled. Escalators, elevators, and ramps that recognize the needs of people in wheelchairs are not part of the design.

Even in the provision of community-based programs in schools, churches, and mosques, the disabled are usually left out. While, in recent times, social attitudes and policies toward the disabled are shifting, the change has not gone far enough, especially in developing countries. In Nigeria, education, which should be a vehicle for breaking the myth surrounding disability, is still inaccessible to the majority of citizens. Education unfortunately has not accomplished much to dispel the superstitious beliefs which follow a person with a disability. Through education, genuine care, and socialization, however, disabilities would no longer be attributed to the whims of evil spirits, but rather to verifiable factors.

Although disability studies before the early 1960s were limited to public attitude surveys and general observations of the behavior of people with disabilities, these studies nevertheless served as a foundation and reference source for several other types of research. The works of Barker (1980), Goffman (1963), and Wright (1960) are examples of such initial studies. These works suggest that disabled people suffer from public prejudice, stereotypy, devaluation, and other status problems that minority groups also experience. Similar to these cited works are various studies conducted by Lukoff and Whitman (1990), who concluded that attitudes toward a disability (blindness) are not the same thing as and thus must be distinguished from attitudes toward the disabled (the blind individual) and that public attitudes toward the disabled are neither uniformly negative nor positive; these attitudes vary with different people and, perhaps, with different environments. Studies have been conducted to uncover dynamics that underlie or are associated with the different ways in which different individuals react to the disabled person (p.373-376).

Studies by Chesler (1995), Fine (1998), Follansee (1990), Marinellia and Kelz (1973), Siller, Chipman, Ferguson, and Vann (1984), and literature reviews by Cloerkes (1981) and Siller (1984), all indicate a clear relationship between these variables and attitudes toward persons with disabilities. However, the correlation between the identified variables and attitudinal behaviors is mostly low, suggesting that disposition variables should not be exclusively relied upon to predict attitudes (Siller, 1984). This correlation corroborates with the point emphasized by Sloat and Frankel (1972): that a disability attitude is a function not of a single factor alone but of several interacting factors of the environment and of the personal qualities of the individual with the attitude.

Odom (1997) describes attitude as a motivational mental set which functions at the level of interests, preferences, wants, values, and beliefs, rather than of a direct satisfaction of needs. Sherif and Sherif (1991) suggest that attitudes imply a relationship between a person and objects, and operate in relation to identifiable referents, whether persons, groups, institutions, objects, values, social issues, or ideologies. To measure attitude, Rosenberg and Robert (1992) developed a schematic conception of attitude as divided into the three components noted earlier: cognitive, affective, and behavioral.

The cognitive component is used by humans in thinking about attitude objects. Categories are inferred from consistencies in response to different stimuli. The affective component is the emotional aspect which changes the idea: for example, pity for or fear of the disabled. If people feel good or bad when they think about the category or attitude object, one could say that they have a positive or negative affect toward the members of the category. Finally, the behavioral component is a predisposition to action, such as avoidance, support, cooperation, or rejection. Attitudes may be conceptualized as organized and habitual ways of thinking, feeling, and reacting to events, objects, and persons (Lambert & Lambert, 1995).

Attitudes help a person understand the world by organizing and simplifying complex inputs from the environment. They play a dominant role in determining behavior and affecting the judgments and perceptions of others. They protect the individual's self-esteem by making it possible to avoid unpleasant truths about oneself. Attitudes are reflected in the philosophies by which an individual lives (Lambert & Lambert, 1994; Triandis & Tanaka, 1999).

While attitudes are acquired through exposure to other attitudes, objects, or referents (e.g., other people, groups, social issues), Triandis (1984) suggests that only a small proportion of attitudes is developed through firsthand experience. Other people are the primary source of information for attitude formation. According to Allport (1995), the majority of a person's attitudes is usually acquired from family and friends.

The child generates personal attitudes and values through interaction with significant others in the environment. According to Parsons (1994), socialization is vital in this process. Both Parsons and Khalfan and Marinell (1998) describe socialization as the process by which the individual develops through interaction with others in specific patterns of socially relevant behavior. Ackerman (1994) identifies the emergence of values and socialization as parallel processes.

A significant aspect of the formation of attitudes and values is the social environment in which the child is reared. Mussen (1996) suggests that each society has a distinctive culture, a particular pattern of motives, ways of thinking, attitudes, and goals which children growing up in that culture acquire. This view supports Parsons and Bales's (1995) concept that an individual's personality is a mirror image of a succession of social systems into which it has been integrated and organized over a requisite series of stages. Mussen (1996) emphasizes that the culture in which the child grows up considerably prescribes the methods and goals of socialization (e.g., how the child will be trained and which personality characteristics, motives, attitudes, and values will be emphasized). Thus, the family in which the child is reared usually has the greatest impact on that child's personality development.

The family is the group to which the child refers in evaluating his own behavior and the behavior of others; the formation of attitudes is integral to the process of forming a self-concept. In fact through the establishment of a constellation of subject-object relationships, the self-concept is delineated. Through this process the group in which the child is born becomes not merely external realities to which he must adapt but reference groups with which he identifies or strives to identify himself (Sherif & Sherif, 1971, p. 299).

Results of a cross-cultural study of childrearing practices by Asch and Odom (1996) suggest that social behavior, dictated by the socioeconomic factors and family structure imbedded in the culture's value system, was transmitted to the child by the age of six. Families participate directly within the larger society in a number of subcultures, including social class, ethnic, language, and religious groups. These aspects of the larger society are most directly available to the child through example, teaching, and daily activities, and are assumed to be part of a particular lifestyle (Elkin & Handle, 1994).

Other investigators who have contributed to public-attitude studies have examined the effect of stimulus used in a study as well as rater characteristics on the outcome of an attitude research. Golin's (1970) study and an investigation by Richardson, Sherif, Robert, and Douglas (1966) are examples of the type of research in reference. In Golin's study, 144 student subjects rated a given attitude object using the following semantic adjectives: valuable-worthless, warm-cold, neat-sloppy, employable-nonemployable, and so forth. The attitude object was introduced as either a physically disabled or an ex-psychiatric patient or nondisabled; with either only a little information or an abundance of information; and with the presented descriptive information made favorable toward the object. Each subject thus responded to the semantic instrument under one of twelve treatment conditions. The results showed that favorableness of information influenced the respondents' attitudes and that, under the conditions examined, attitudes toward people with disability were as favorable as or even more favorable than attitudes toward the nondisabled. Indeed, where brief unfavorable information was presented, attitudes were more positive toward people with disability than toward the nondisabled control.

Richardson et al. (1996) examined the effect of rater characteristics on attitude valence. Hundreds of ten- and eleven-year-old children with diverse backgrounds were tested for their preference ranking of six stimulus pictures; one showed a nondisabled child, and each of the five others depicted a child with some type of physical handicap. Despite race, sex, socioeconomic status, and other similar characteristics, the rater subjects showed a high preference for the normal child, a lesser preference for people with mild disabilities, and the least preference for people with disabilities whose appearance was less attractive. From this rater's consistency in ranking, the investigators concluded the existence of a cultural uniformity in reactions to persons with physical disabilities.

Follow-up studies and replications of the 1961 investigation yielded data that supported the initial findings (Richardson, 1996). One other source of insight into the nature of public attitudes is the attitude research that examined not only a particular group, but also comparable other groups or various segments of which a group is composed. Two such research studies, cited below, contribute some of the clearest findings on public attitudes.

To ascertain the attitudes harbored toward the deaf individual by different age groups within the American culture, Horowitz, Ree, and Horowitz (1992) administered attitude questionnaires to five groups composed of twenty subjects each: sixth-grade pupils, high school students, undergraduate students, graduate students, and members of a parent-teacher association. The results showed that the five groups formed a continuum of increasing maturity and sophistication in attitudes concerning the respondents' views on the deaf's personal and achievement characteristics. The groups, however, did not differ in their views on training the deaf and how to treat the deaf individual. Gottlieb and Corman (1998) administered attitude instruments to a population of 430 respondents to measure awareness—through semantic differential and attitudinal rating—and to appraise public acceptance of retarded children. The results showed that on some scale items, respondents were massively positive in attitudes while not so on other items; and some segment of the population evidenced more favorability than others on given issues. Whereas 88 percent of the respondents agreed that parents ought to allow their normal children to play with a retarded peer, the population was fairly evenly divided on the three response alternatives—agree, disagree, unsure—regarding whether the retarded child should be educated in a special class. In addition, older respondents—parents of school-age children and persons who previously had contact with the retarded—were more inclined to favor segregation of retarded children in the community.

While these studies provide valuable insight into the nature of public attitudes, it is unclear why the findings differ so radically among many of the cited studies. In particular as well as collectively, the results obtained by Golin (1970), Richardson et al. (1961), Horowitz, Rees, and Horowitz (1992), and Gottlieb and Corman (1998) indicate that public attitudes toward the disabled are sometimes positive, sometimes negative, and sometimes neutral or mixed. However, one cannot yet confidently pinpoint which factors lead to which attitude propensity. Is it the particular conditions which the investigator experimentally creates; the type of attitude instrument used in a study; the nature of social intercourse with the disabled which the attitude subjects perceived was implicated in the study exercise; among other possibilities?

Even more difficult to evaluate are any effects the instruments may have had on the study outcome, because most of these studies, understandably so, used nonstandardized scales whose psychometric properties were usually not reported. Based on the assumption that people with disabilities cannot care for themselves, many were institutionalized or in nursing homes, while others were excluded by inaccessible buildings or by people without disabilities who regarded them as subhuman (Robert, 1994; Rodde, 1999). Legal reforms have attempted to counter these trends. To date, the most sweeping reform has been the Americans with Disabilities Act of 1990, which acknowledges that historically, society has tended to isolate and segregate individuals with disabilities, and despite some improvements, such forms of discrimination against individuals who have experienced discrimination on the basis of race, color, sex, national origin, or age, individuals who have experienced discrimination on the basis of disability have often had no legal recourse to redress such discrimination (U.S. Congress, 1990).

By contrast, Nigeria's experience with democratic rule began in the 1950s, when both the British and Nigerians wanted to create an independent Nigeria that would be ruled by a multiparty Western-type democracy. That parliamentary experiment lasted just over five years, from October 1960 to January 1966. On January 15, 1966, the first republic was overthrown by a group of military personnel. Their intention was a radical and nationalist protest against the tribalism and corruption of the politicians. On May 27, 1967, then president Gowon announced the creation of twelve states, which finally gave the minorities their place in the society. At that point, the Nigerian civil war broke out between the Northerners and the Ibos (Biafra) from the eastern part of Nigeria.

The war lasted from 1967 to 1970. On January 15, 1970, the Ibos (Biafrans) surrendered unconditionally. In 1970-74, the second Educational Developmental Plan was put forward; according to this social ideal, "a just and egalitarian society puts a premium on reducing inequalities in inter-personal incomes and promoting balanced development among the various communities . . . it organizes its economic institutions in such a way that there is no oppression based on class, social status, ethnic group or state" (p. 17).

In late July 1975, Gowon's government was overthrown in a bloodless coup. Soon thereafter, Brigadier Murtala Ramat Muhammed, who led the Nigerians for 201 days, was assassinated on February 13, 1976. The task of governing Nigeria fell to his army chief of staff, General Olusegun Obasanjo. By 1977, the problem of identity remained unresolved and haunted every aspect of national life.

Two years later, in 1979, Alhaji Shehu Shagari was elected a civilian president. His leadership ended by 1983, and this period marked the end of the second republic. The members of the opposition parties called on the military to overthrow the Shagari government. Following the Shagari presidency was sixteen years of military rule, featuring such corrupt dictators as Ibrahim Babangida and Sani Abacha—a span of time which eroded the tradition of federalism in Nigeria.

In May 1999, President Olusegun Obasanjo was inaugurated to a four-year term after winning elections in February of that year. The Nigerian constitution provided for an independent judiciary. Although the judicial branch remained susceptible to executive- and legislative-branch pressures, the performance of the Supreme Court and decisions at the federal level indicated growing independence. State and local judiciary were influenced by political leaders and suffered from corruption and inefficiency more so than the court system.

This political inconsistency resulted in inadequate infrastructure, endemic corruption, and general economic mismanagement hindering economic growth. A significant percentage of the country's population lived in poverty and was subject to malnutrition and disease. Hence, the government's human rights record remained poor; despite improvements in several areas, serious problems continued. Shari'a courts sentenced persons to harsh punishment including amputations and death by stoning, while prison conditions were harsh and life-threatening. Domestic violence against women remained widespread, and some forms were even sanctioned by traditional, customary or Shari'a law. For example, Amina Lawal, a Nigerian peasant woman, was sentenced to death by stoning for committing adultery by the Shari'a court, even though she was separated from her husband at that point. Her pregnancy was used as evidence of her crime, inherently discriminating against Ms. Lawal's right. Her actions had violated an important tenet of Islamic thought: that "men and women are not equal." The verdict before the law proved otherwise because of worldwide pressure. When or where the situation will end is uncertain.

Discrimination against women and people with disabilities remained a problem. Specifically, female genital mutilation was widely practiced in some parts of the country, and child abuse, child prostitution, and child labor were common. People with disabilities were not seen as equal to other children; they were widely disregarded as capable of and needing love, affection, humor, friendship, cultural, artistic expression, and intellectual stimulation People with disabilities were segregated, marginalized, isolated, and subjected to physical and sexual violence with relative impunity. They are usually defined by what they lack rather than what they have. In general, though, this process not only dehumanizes people with disabilities but also dehumanizes society.

In Nigeria, there is evidence of the negative side of these positive correlations between rights, beliefs, and attitudes toward disabilities. The educational system in Nigeria has witnessed a very different history of equal treatment of people with disabilities and some individuals regarded as outcasts, "Osu." The human rights group outlined the atrocities meted out against the Osu in Igbo land. They include parents poison of children by parents, disinheritance, ostracism, organized attack, heaping harvest offering separately in churches, denial of membership in social clubs, violent disruption of marriage ceremonies, denial of chieftaincy titles, deprivation of property, and expulsion of wives. The Osu were believed to be dedicated to the gods and were shunned by others as "horrible and unholy." The Osu caste discrimination is very pronounced in the area of marriage. An Osu cannot marry a freeborn. The belief is that any freeborn that marries an Osu defiles the family. So, freeborn families are always up in arms against any of their members who want to marry an Osu. They go to any length to abort the plan. Because of the Osu factor, marriages in Igbo land are preceded by investigations—elders on both sides travel to native villages to find out the social status of the other party. They could only marry other Osu. The Osu are regarded as slaves, strangers, untouchables, and outcasts. Being an Osu is like leprosy in the minds of the Igbos. The Osu system is practiced among the people from the eastern part of Nigeria, the Igbos. This system is still in existence even with impact of Christianity, modern education, civilization, and the onset of the human rights culture. The question is, why is it that this cultural disease, practices has refused to go away even among educated Igbo people. The Osu's are asked to live at a separate/isolated location and treated as inferior human beings in a state of permanent and irreversible disability and stigma. The reason is because the Igbo people are a very religious and theistic people and the practice of Osu system is hinged on religion, supernaturalism, and theism.

The Osu are regarded as unclean or untouchable because they are dedicated to the gods. So it is the dedication to the gods that makes the Osu status a condition of permanent and irreversible disability and stigma. Within each culture there are also internal tensions and pressures. It is mostly subculture and nondominant sections of the community that mount challenges to dominant culture. One such cultural practice under challenge has been, and continues to be, the concept of "Osu caste." Igbo people continue to expose the inequities arising out of Osu, and this has led to the outcry of some well-meaning Igbo people voicing the atrocity associated to this caste system.

Before the arrival or involvement of missionaries and voluntary agencies in education in Nigeria, people with disabilities were relegated to the most abhorrent position in the society, primarily because of superstition. For instance, a child born without arms or with hands protruding from the elbows poses many unanswerable questions (especially to the uninformed) about the reasons for this physical deformity.

Special education is a new phenomenon in the Nigerian educational system, and tremendous efforts have been made to improve the socioeconomic and educational structures of the country. However, the general system has problems in establishing a suitable philosophy that would reflect all the basic structures of the system.

In 1975, Mrs. Ruth Ogbue (then in charge of Special Education Unit of the Federal Ministry of Education, Lagos, Nigeria) began reviewing the special education facilities in Nigeria. According to her, "at present, there is no national policy on special education"; therefore, the responsibility for special education is left to the discretion of the individual states. Even where the education laws of the states mention special education, they provide no definite mandate for people with disabilities. Since Nigerian independence in (1960), Section 8 of the National Policy on Education (1977) made provisions for policy direction for special education. Problems resulting from cultural influences on special education were identified as low level of parenthood literacy, superstitions, taboos of ethnic cultures, lack of parental involvement, absence of legislation protecting people with special needs, and unstable political influence, which impede the development of an orderly system of special education.

Treatment of People with Disabilities: Retention of Culture as Inequity in Nigeria

Too often the experiences of people with disability are denied, discounted, and trivialized, leading to a sense of frustration and powerlessness. The experience of some disability in the Igbo culture is that of the subtlety of racism in interpersonal relations with many able-bodied people. Racism refers not only to the prejudice and discriminatory treatment actually experienced. The marginalizing experiences range from exclusion from activities involving use of voice, being prejudicially termed disabled, to difficulty finding jobs. Their experiences include being belittled, being ostracized, segregated in relation to education, and low expectations.

In Ibo land, social attitudes toward the disabled persons in general have been slow in changing. The disabled were believed to be the "root of social evils" and a burden to civilization (Abang, 1992; Oni, 1982). However, in the modern democracy, freedom and inclusion are ideals at the core of the value system. While the modern democracy claims to treat all persons equally, the poor, disabled, and minority groups have historically been neglected, mistreated, and socially isolated. All of these groups yearn for their rights. They wanted to have the same opportunities for living optimally that more advantaged members of the society have experienced. The freedom ideal, which states that every person has the right to determine his or her direction in life, and the inclusion ideal, which states that every person has a right to be included in society, have attempted to allow the disenfranchised attainment of these benefits.

Educational provisions for disabled individuals have lagged behind the education of their nondisabled peers in every country and, frequently, by hundreds of years. The history of special education in Africa, and in Nigeria in particular, is for the most part a reenactment of the trends elsewhere in the world, with a dramatic governmental interest rising in 1974. Although the legislative basis for special education dates back to 1810 in Australia, 1961 in Brazil, 1901 in Argentina, and 1945 in Iran, the earliest law in Nigeria mentioning educational provisions for people with disabilities was the Lagos Education Act of 1957, which merely called for organization of special education in Lagos if and when necessary. Despite these isolated laws, most of the early schools for people with disabilities were established by Christian missionaries. In postcolonial Nigerian politics, the concept of "bringing government closer to the people" originates from at least three sources that support the goal of decentralizing the structure of the state through the creation of ever-smaller administrative units. These sources are the Nigerian people, the state, and the World Bank, the premier multilateral organization that has come to dominate policymaking on both political and economic development in the countries of the third world. To argue that the state is a source of the concept is also to argue that the origins of the contemporary conceptualization of decentralization are colonial. This is because Nigeria's postcolonial state inherited the mores and ethos of its colonial predecessor and thus continues colonial traditions such as federalization through the creation of smaller administrative units. In this tradition, three regions were created in 1954. After Nigeria's independence in 1960, the number increased to four when the midwest region was created in 1963. In 1967, twelve states were created to replace the regions. In 1976, seven states were created. Two states were created in 1987. In 1991, nine states were created. And in 1996, more states were created. There are thirty-six states in the federation of Nigeria. Paradoxically, this mode of decentralization neither brings the government closer to the people nor quells the ardent demands from communities that ask for equitable regional or ethnic representation. "Ironically, instead of making a frontal assault against the inequities and inequalities that plague Nigeria, dealing with uneven devolution of power between the federal, state, and local governments, and responding to the marginalization of some citizens in favor of others, what decentralization does, in the creation of states, is continues—like colonial rule before it—to incorporate the majority of the population as subjects, not citizens."

Today, Nigeria is struggling with these democratic ideals. Recently, its treatment of one of its citizens who was accused of adultery (Amina Lawal, cited earlier) and other practices raise questions about human rights. Under the Shari'a court, a person who steals can be punished by amputation. These violations reinforce the belief that people with deformities are guilty of some crime against the community. Some barriers encountered are physical, but more often they are attitudinal. It is also likely that many of the physical barriers are due to negative attitudes, lack of knowledge, rejection of rights, and misconceptions. Some of the negative attitudes are concerned with supernatural beliefs about causes of disability and misconceptions about its effects, with disability stereotypes playing a large role in the way persons with disability are perceived by the public.

Many studies have focused on identifying techniques that produce attitudinal change toward people with disabilities. The results of these studies have varied (Donaldson,1980). For instance, when direct contact with people with disabilities was structured, in most studies, there was a consistent positive attitude change (MacHale & Simeonson, 1980, Voeltz, 1982). What this means is that interactions between people with disabilities and people without disabilities were carefully planned so that they would increase sensitivity, awareness, and communication skills between the participants with and without disabilities. For unstructured contacts, there have been mixed findings where sometimes there were positive attitudinal shifts and sometimes there were negative attitudinal shifts. It has been suggested that nonstructural experiences may expose people with disabilities in stereotypic manners that reinforce negative stereotypes (Donaldson, 1980). Attitudes toward people with disabilities are difficult to change.

The traditional approach of the Nigerian populations toward people with disabilities has overly emphasized the pained effect and is essentially negative. Negative stereotypes and beliefs, emotions, and behaviors toward people with disabilities pose a significant obstacle and are associated with disabling conditions and positive beliefs about what all people deserve regardless to cope with rejection by elements of their environment in addition to possible difficulties in personal adjustment to the disabling conditions. Certain beliefs have been closely associated with formation of attitudes toward the disabled. These include the belief about body-whole, body-beautiful (Wright, 1960), which extols the value of perfect physique and the implied difference between perfect and imperfect physique. Prejudice against people with disabilities in this part of the world been found to be associated with cultural beliefs, policies, laws, cultural modernities, and cultural norms that attach great importance to health, behavior, and appearance and also to the degree of cultural modernities (Schneider and Anderson, 1980). The implicit theory (Schneider, 1975) attempts to associate certain human traits with certain predictable outcomes. For instance, a disabled body has a disabled mind. The just-world phenomenon (Lerner, 1975), holds that the world is a just and fair place; any person who does good will receive goodness and those suffering, deprived, and disabled deserve their fate. Public awareness of the civil rights movement for this population remains limited, and the stereotyping of people with developmental disabilities as noncontributing citizens who are dependent on others remain common. Disability is a reality for millions of people across the world. Living with disability implies actively living, a goal society must strive to achieve. In order for that to happen, we must examine the issues, question policies, and organize to ensure that people with disabilities everywhere are given the same rights and access to opportunities. Thinking through ideas and writing what you know is a critical step. We must begin to envision a new society where people can live and interact, marry and be married, elect and be elected, without division, distinction, or discrimination on the basis of identity or disability.

References

Abang, T. B. (1992). Special education in Nigeria. *International Journal Disability, Development and Education, 39,* 13-18.

Abeng, B., and R. Stancliffe, (1996). The ecology of self-determination. In M. L. Wehmeyer and D. J. Sands (Eds.), *Self-determination across the life span: Independence and choice for people with disabilities.* Baltimore: Paul H. Brooke.

Baker, J. L., and J.Gottlieb, (1980). Attitudes of teachers toward mainstreaming retarded children. In J. Gottlieb (Ed.), *Educating mentally retarded persons in the mainstream* (pp. 450__-520__). Baltimore: University Park Press.

Brown, F., Belz, P., Corsi, L., and B. Wenig, (1993). Choice diversity for people with severe disabilities. *Journal of Education and Training in Mental Retardation, 10,* 79-86.

Cloerkes, G. (1981). Are prejudices against disabled persons determined by personality characteristics? *International Review of Rehabilitation Research, 4,* 35-46.

Clore, G. L., and K. Jeffrey, (1972). Emotional role playing, attitude change, and attraction toward a disabled person. *Journal of Personality and Social Psychology, 23,* 40-45.

Cohen, B. S. (1991). *A comparison of self-concept scores in secondary aged hearing impaired students enrolled in mainstreamed and self-contained classes.* Unpublished doctoral dissertation, Pace University.

Cohen, O. (1990). Deaf children from ethnic, linguistic and racial minority backgrounds: An overview. *American Annals of the Deaf, 135*, 67-73.

Cohen, S., and F. Brown, (1993). Self-determination and young children. In M. L. Wehmeyer and D. J. Sands (Eds.), *Self-determination across the life span: Independence and choice for people with disabilities*. Baltimore: Paul H. Brooke.

Corman, L., and J. Gottlieb, (1998). Mainstreaming mentally retarded children: A review of research. In N. R. Ellis (Ed.), *International review of research in mental retardation (Vol. 9)*. New York: Academic Press.

Crandell, J. M. (1969). The genesis and modification of attitudes toward the child who is different. *Training School Bulletin, 66*, 72-79.

Diamond, L. (1984, Spring). *Nigeria in search of democracy*. Foreign Affairs, Council on Foreign Relations, Inc.

Donaldson, R., Helmstetter, B., Donaldson, J., and R. West, (1994). *Influencing high school students' attitudes toward and interactions with peers with disabilities*.

Evans, J. H. (1996). Changing attitudes toward disabled persons: An experimental study. *Rehabilitation Counseling Bulletin*.

Facia, C. (1994). Curse or divine wrath. *UNESCO Sources, 59*, 4.

Favazza, P. L., and S. L. Odom, (1997). Promoting positive attitudes of kindergarten-age children toward people with disabilities.

Federal Republic of Nigeria. (1981). *National policy on education (revised)*. Yaba-Lagos, Nigeria: NERC Press.

Field, S., and A.Hoffman, (1996). Promoting self-determination in school reform: Individualized planning and curriculum efforts. In D. J. M. L. Sands Wehmeyer (Eds.), *Self-determination across the life span: Independence and choice for people with disabilities* (pp. 197-213). Baltimore: Paul H. Brookes Publishing Company.

Furnham, A., and M. Gibbs, (1984). School children's attitudes towards the handicapped. *Journal of Adolescence, 7*, 99-117.

Gilhool, T. K. (1997, May). Education: An inalienable right. *Exceptional Children, 39*(8), 603.

Golin, A. K. (1970). Stimulus variables in the measurement of attitudes toward disability. *Rehabilitation Counseling Bulletin, 14*, 20-26.

Gottlieb, J., B. W.Gottlieb, (1997). Stereotypic attitudes and behavioral intentions toward handicapped children. *American Journal of Mental Deficiency, 82.*

Hazzard, A. (1983). Children's experience with knowledge of attitude toward disabled persons. *The Journal of Special Education, 17* (2), 131-139.

Hoffman, A., S. Field, (1995). Promoting self-determination through effective curriculum development. *Intervention in School and Clinic, 30*, 133-141.

Horowitz, L. S., Ree, N. S., M. W.Horowitz, (1965). Attitudes toward deafness as a function of increasing maturity. *Journal of Social Psychology, 66*, 331-336.

Humana, C. (1992). *World human rights guide.* New York: Oxford University Press.

Isiches, E. A. (1929). *A history of Africa since 1800.* London: Allen University.

Khalfan, H. K. (1993). Disability and literacy. *AHRTAG, 16*, 4-5.

Langer, E. J., Fiske, S., Taylor, S. E., & Chanowitz, B. (1976). Stigma, string, and discomfort: A novel-stimulus hypothesis. *Journal of Experimental and Social Psychology, 12*, 451-463.

Mba, P. O. (1978). Attitudes towards handicapped in developing countries and steps towards attitudinal changes. Paper presented at the First World Congress on the Future of Special Education, University of Stirling, Scotland.

McHale, S. M., R. Simeonsson, (1980). Effects of interaction on nonhandicapped children's attitudes toward autistic children. *American Journal of Mental Deficiency, 85* (1), 18-24.

Mithaug, D. E. (1991). *Self-determined kids: Raising satisfied and successful children.* Lexington, MA: D. C. Heath and Company.

Mithaug, D. E. (1996a). *Equal opportunity theory.* Thousand Oaks, CA: Sage Publications.

Mithaug, D. E. (1996b). The optimal prospects principle: A theoretical basis for rethinking instructional practices for self-determination. In M. L. Wehmeyer & D. J. Sands (Eds.), *Self-determination across the life span: Independence and choice for people with disabilities* (pp. 147-165). Baltimore: Paul H. Brooke.

Mithaug, D. E. (1996c). TE5010, Study Problems/Issues—Special Education. Course materials, Teachers College, Columbia University, New York.

Mithaug, D. E. (1997). TE6002, Administration—Special Education Programs. Course materials, Teachers College, Columbia University, New York.

Mithaug, D. E., Martin, J. E., Agran, M., and F. R. Rusch, (1988). *Why special education graduates fail.* Colorado Springs, CO: Ascent Publication.

Murray-Seegert, C. (Special needs in the classroom. 1994. *UNESCO Sources* 59: 7-8. 1986). *Nasty girls, thugs, and humans like us: Social relations between severely disabled and nondisabled students in high school.* Baltimore: Paul H. Brooke.

Newman, R. K., R.L. Simpson, (1983). Modifying the least restrictive environment to facilitate the integration of severely emotionally disturbed children and youth. *Behavioral Disorders, 8* (2),103-112.

Nieves-Jorrel, R. (1983). Parents' attitudes and social competence of the mentally handicapped child in Puerto Rico. *Dissertation Abstracts International, 43*, 10.

Nwabuzor, E. J. "Profile of Women in Nigerian Politics during the Transition," in J.A.A. Ayodele, et al, eds. Women and Politics in Nigeria, Lagos; Malthouse Press, 1992:77-103.

Ogbu, R. M. (1975). *A survey of special education facilities in Nigeria.* Lagos, Nigeria: Federal Ministry of Nigeria.

Reis, E. (1988). Improving attitudes of nonretarded fourth graders toward people who are mildly mentally retarded: Implications for mainstreaming. *Education and Training of the Mentally Retarded, 23*, 85-91.

Shapiro, J. P. (1993). *No pity: People with disabilities forging a new civil rights movement.* New York: Times Books.

Shaver, J. P., Curtis, C. K., Jesunathadas, J., C. J.Strong, (1987). The modification of attitudes toward people with disabilities: Is there a best way? *Internaitonal Journal of Special Education, 4*, 33-57.

Siller, J. (1984). The role of personality in attitudes toward those with physical disabilities. In _R.L., Jones, (Ed.), *Current topics in rehabilitation psychology* (pp.184-204). New York: Grune & Stratton.

Siller, J. (1970). Disability factor scales-general. Unpublished document, New York University.

Simpson, R., Parrish, N., and J., Cook, (1976). Modification of attitudes of regular class children towards the handicapped for the purpose of achieving integration. *Contemporary Educational Psychology, 1*, 46-51.

Siperstein, G. N. (1996). *Instruments for measuring children's attitudes toward the handicapped*. Unpublished manuscript, University of Massachusetts.

Special needs in the classroom. (1994). *UNESCO Sources, 59*, 7-8.

"The Status of State Governments in Nigeria's Federalism." Publius: The Journal of Federalism 24 Summer 1992: 181-200.

Triandis, H. C. (1971). *Attitude and attitude change*. New York: John Wiley & Sons.

UNESCO. (1995). *The state of the world's children*. New York: Oxford University Press.

Voeltz, L. M. (1982). Effects of structured interactions with severely handicapped peers of children's attitudes. *American Association on Mental Deficiency, 82* (4), 380-390.

Vurdelja-Maglajlic, D., and J. E. Jordan, (1974). Attitude-behavior toward retardation of mothers of retarded and non-retarded in four nations. *The Training School Bulletin, 71*, 17-29.

Wehmayer, M. L. (1995). A career education approach: Self-determination for youth with mild cognitive disabilities. *Intervention in School and Clinic, 30*, 157-163.

Wehmeyer, M. L., and D.J. Sands, (1996). Future directions in self-determination: Articulating values and policies, recognizing organizational structures and implementing professional practices. In M. L. Wehmeyer and D. J. Sands (Eds.), *Self-determination across the life span: Independence and choice for people with disabilities* (pp. 3-16). Baltimore: Paul H. Brooke.

Weiner, B. (1993). On sin versus sickness: A theory of perceived responsibility and social motivation. *American Psychologist, 48*, 957-965.

Weller, L., Costeff, C., Cohen, B., D. Rahman,. (1974). Social variables in perception and acceptance of retardation. *American Journal of Mental Deficiency, 79*, 274-278.

Whitman, T. J. (1990). Development of self-regulation in persons with mental retardation. *American Journal on Mental Retardation, 94*, 373-376.

Wolfensberger, W., R., Kurtz,. (1971). A measurement of parents' perception of their children's development. *Genetic Psychology Monographs, 83*, 3-92.

Wright, B. A. (1973). *Physical disability: A psychological approach*. New York: Harper and Row.

Yuker, H. E. (1994). Variables that influence attitudes toward people with disabilities: Conclusions from the data. *Journal of Social Behavior and Personality, 9* (5), 2-22

About The Author

Josephine Uzoamaka Aguoji has earned a doctorate degree in Administration and Supervision of Special Education Programs and a Master's degree in Early Childhood Special Education from Teacher's College, Columbia University.

She has a degree in Educational Administration from the University of Lagos Nigeria and a Bachelors degree in English Language/ Education from Bayero University, Kano, Nigeria.

She is an educator at heart; she has worked with Board of Education in different capacities, both as a reading and classroom teacher, and a Supervisor.

Currently she is lecturing at Medgar Evers College, Brooklyn, New York as an Assistant Adjunct Professor.

www.ingramcontent.com/pod-product-compliance
Lightning Source LLC
Chambersburg PA
CBHW061229280526
45784CB00006B/2691